All Alone:
Surviving the Loss of
Your Spouse

Kathleen Rawlings Buntin

Deseret Book Company
Salt Lake City, Utah

Library of Congress Cataloging-in-Publication Data
  Buntin, Kathleen Rawlings.
    [Living half]
    All alone : surviving the loss of your spouse / Kathleen Rawlings
  Buntin.
      p.   cm.
    Originally published: The Living half, c1984.
    ISBN 0-87579-933-7
    1. Bereavement—Religious aspects—Christianity. 2. Buntin,
  Kathleen Rawlings. I. Title.
  BV4908.B86   1995
  248.8'6—dc20
                                               94-40691
                                               CIP

Printed in the United States of America

10   9   8   7   6   5   4   3   2   1

To Carmon because . . .

Contents

CONTENTS

Acknowledgments

Many people played important roles in helping me with the preparation and writing of this book. Special thanks to the following:

Ken Groscost and Jan Belknap, both teachers, counselors, and friends.

Sharon Jones, my Relief Society visiting teacher, and her husband, Gary, and Harold Payne, my home teacher, and his wife, Barbara—all of whom have magnified their callings with honor.

Charlene Taylor, my friend, editor, typist, and confidante. She made what was good better.

Sharon and Jay Whitmore, who encouraged me and gave me confidence that I had something of value to say.

My brother, Brent Rawlings, and my sisters, Darlene Richards and Nancy Johnson, and their families, who were all excited about the book and kept me excited too.

My mother, Hazel Rawlings, who is my true confidante, my dear, sweet friend.

My father, G. Barney Rawlings, my mentor and my first and finest critic.

My children—Brian, Shawn, Terri, and Shane—who went through a lot with me and who, despite their own pain and loss, have been a comfort and a support.

My children-in-law, Mary, Retta, Stacey, and Mitchell, and my grandchildren, who make me smile again.

Prologue

And Adam said, This is now bone of my bones, and flesh of my flesh: she shall be called Woman, because she was taken out of Man. Therefore shall a man leave his father and his mother, and shall cleave unto his wife: and they shall be one flesh.

Genesis 2:23–24

AUGUST 29, 1982

The telephone rang at a quarter to six that Sunday morning. I was sleeping very soundly, which was unusual. I generally experienced a certain restless insomnia whenever Carmon was away on a hunting trip, as he had been since Thursday. It took several rings before the sound pierced my deep slumber. I reached for the phone beside my bed. "Hello?" My speech sounded thick and groggy to me.

"Mrs. Buntin?" It was a woman's voice that I did not recognize. "This is the Gilbert Police Department. A sheriff's deputy is on his way to talk to you. I don't know what it's about, but we need directions to your house. All we have is a rural route number."

I gave the directions calmly, then hung up the phone and swung my feet out of bed. I started to reach for my robe. All the while my brain was mentally shaking itself awake, trying to decide how much alarm to register. "No," I thought, "I'd better get dressed." I left the robe lying on the foot of my bed. "If Carm's been hurt or had a heart attack (he had worn a pacemaker for over a year), I'll want to go to him quickly."

I reached instead for the skirt and blouse I had worn the day before. I didn't bother with hose, but slipped my bare feet into my shoes. Then I headed for the bathroom to brush my teeth and wash my face. I used the company bathroom rather than the one off our bedroom so as not to awaken my eight-year-old son, who was sleeping beside me. "Time enough for that when I leave for the hospital," I thought.

I was just combing my hair when the front doorbell rang. "The deputy must have been close by. He sure got here quickly," I said to myself.

I opened the door. There on the front porch stood two men, one a uniformed officer, the other wearing jeans and a shirt. "Mrs. Buntin? I have some very bad news for you. Your husband, Carmon, has been killed in an automobile accident."

Just like that. No buildup, no beating around the bush, no softening of the blow. Just the facts, ma'am.

Time slipped out of sync . . .

" . . . and they twain shall be one flesh." (Matthew 19:5.) One flesh . . . two parts making one whole . . . and now, I was all alone.

CHAPTER ONE

Why?

Oh that my grief were throughly weighed, and my calamity laid in the balances together!

Let the day perish wherein I was born, and the night in which it was said, There is a man child conceived.

Oh that I might have my request; and that God would grant me the thing that I long for! Even that it would please God to destroy me.

Job 6:2; 3:3; 6:8–9

*W*e are a death-denying society. We put our sick people into hospitals and our aged into "homes." Americans are more comfortable discussing sex explicitly than talking about death. Until it hits close to home, death is one of those things we hope will go away if we keep our heads in the sand long enough. That is understandable, for to contemplate the reality of anyone's death is to come face-to-face with our own finiteness and mortality. John Donne said it well when he wrote, "Never send to know for whom the bell tolls; / It tolls for thee."

Death is a fact of life as surely as is birth. When we find ourselves in the valley of its shadow, we can no longer avoid that ultimate taboo. No matter what euphemisms are employed—"passed away," "asleep," "gone on to his reward"—sooner or later, the hard reality hits us all that he (or she) is gone forever from this life and is not coming back.

In the Church we receive a lot of comfort in knowing where the dead person is. There is anticipation and joy in the knowledge that families are truly forever. But to the living

spouse, forever is a long way off! Who helps the living understand where they are? Who helps them to cope with their
grief during those endless, empty nights when they ask,
"Why?" and pray to die? Who helps them literally to endure
to the end?

To those unacquainted with grief, it seems that a testimony
of the plan of eternal salvation should be enough to get us
through the process relatively unscathed. It does help, of
course, to have that firm, abiding conviction of a life after
death. (Losing a loved one is very hard on those who see this
life as the total picture, and not as a small part of a larger
whole without beginning or end.) But even with a testimony,
we feel the immensity of our loss and we grieve for that loss,
often not understanding why.

Unfortunately, others, unless they have experienced such
a loss themselves, do not understand either. Altogether too
often, well-meaning family and friends will say and do all
the wrong things. As one woman put it, "It's like being cut
off at the knees and then being told to get up and run the

race anyway." In my personal experience, it was more like being wrenched completely in half and then being told how strong I was and what a good example I was and how I had to "buck up" and "hang in there" and "be patient." When times came (and they did come) when I wasn't strong or patient, when things seemed more than I could bear, and when I fell apart emotionally, I felt like a total failure— a self-indulgent weakling not fit for God or man.

But grief is *not* a luxury. It is not a self-indulgence. It is not a sign of weakness. Grief is a psychological necessity. It is making "real" inside of ourselves an event that has already occurred outside of ourselves. It is teaching the heart what the head already knows. It cannot be forced or consciously controlled or scheduled to a timetable. It is a pain that must be felt and processed. Grief is work.

Those who deny or hide their grief, whether for noble or selfish reasons, are merely postponing the inevitable. The longer the postponement, the worse the ultimate pain.

There are basically five stages of the grieving process

through which survivors pass; all people experience them at their own speed and in their own way.

The first stage of grieving is shock and denial. It can last for twenty-four hours or as long as several weeks. It is followed by guilt, anger, and depression. These stages are not on a clearly defined continuum through which we move at a predictable pace. They fluctuate and overlap; they disappear, only to reappear again when triggered by some memory. They don't happen in the same order or degree for all people, and each person experiences them in his or her own way and time. But each grieving person does experience them, and knowing that they are normal and will pass can help us to understand and to endure.

The final stage in the grieving process is resolution and acceptance. This stage occurs when the mourner can focus his or her energy on the future and not on the past. It is a gradual process, not a one-time miracle. Like the other stages of grieving, it can be reached, only to slip later from our grasp at the sound of a song or the rush of feelings associated with a special day. In many ways, the resolution of grief is like repentance: not something we achieve once and for all but something we seek and reexperience often.

I've seen grief graphically represented as waves washing over the shore, flowing and ebbing like the tides. I've seen it drawn like a loop, constantly recircling upon itself in ever-decreasing spirals. I've heard it described as an emotional roller-coaster ride with high peaks plummeting to low valleys. But whatever picture is most meaningful for each of us, we can rest in the assurance that things do level out and that slowly, almost imperceptibly, the highs last longer and the lows come less frequently.

We can rest also in the knowledge that although letting go and moving forward are the ultimate goals in resolving our grief, those never mean forgetting the one we love.

CHAPTER TWO

No!

Call for the mourning women, that they may come; . . . and let them make haste, and take up a wailing for us, that our eyes may run down with tears, and our eyelids gush out with waters. . . . For death is come up into our windows.

Jeremiah 9:17–18, 21

AUGUST 29, 1982

Time slipped out of sync. "No!" I wanted to say. "You've got it all wrong! That's not the way the scene is supposed to be read. You're supposed to tell me he's hurt; he's in the hospital! You came to take me to him!"

But I didn't say that. I'm not sure what I said. (Later I was to think it was my fault. If I'd only told them no, then Carmon wouldn't be dead. If I'd only not answered the phone, if I'd only not known, then life would have gone on normally, and he would have come home that afternoon as we had planned.)

I opened the door further for the officers, and my husband's dog, Brandi, rushed in. She was not allowed in the house and rarely ever tried it, but now she slipped in and was slinking along the floor on her belly one minute and running berserkly the next.

"Help me catch her," I begged the policemen. "She's got ticks." The man in the jeans caught the dog, and somehow we managed to put her out the door. I felt like a sleepwalker, and everyone looked as though he were moving underwater.

Sounds somehow came out of the fog like a 45-RPM record played on 33 RPM.

"I said, 'Can I call someone to be with you?'" It was Officer Olsen speaking to me.

"Yes, my bishop."

"What's his name and number and I'll call him for you."

"That's okay. I can call myself."

"I'd be happy to call him for you."

"It's okay. I'm okay." Was I shouting? "I can do it!" My brown desk calendar with my list of frequently called numbers was on my desk in the kitchen. The stake phone directory was next to it. I began to fumble through the Phoenix metropolitan phone book.

"Please let me help you. I can call him. What's his name?"

"Ray. Dennis Ray. I'll call him myself. I'm okay." I had the book open, and my eyes swept the guide words at the top of the page. I could see pages of names, but I couldn't read any of them. My eyes, although dry, wouldn't focus. My hands shook as I thumbed through the pages looking for the Rs.

"Please, Mrs. Buntin. Let me call him for you." Gently he took the phone book from my hands.

Shock and denial. Someone once described the shock following the death of a loved one as a cocoon of numbness. When I experienced it, it was hard for me to imagine how anything so excruciatingly painful could be called numb. It was only later, when many of my support systems were withdrawn, that I realized that I had indeed been mercifully cushioned. Painful though it was, there was a sense of unreality about those first twenty-four hours as the family gathered. We wandered around the house like lost children; and although we clung to each other and cried, we were unable to comfort one another. It was as though each of us expected Carmon to walk through the door any minute and ask us why we were all crying.

During this early stage, there is a sense of disbelief and even denial. The more unexpected the loss, the greater the shock, the harder the grief. In fact, denial can go on long after the initial shock has passed. One of my husband's sisters kept insisting that the police had mixed up the wallets and that the other man in the accident was dead. When she actually saw Carmon's body two days later, she became physically ill.

I thought I had escaped the denial pretty well until the night after the funeral. I was emptying garbage cans in the backyard when I looked at the driveway and could almost see his little brown truck pulling in. I remember shouting, "Okay! Enough is enough! I've played your little game of pain, now send him home!"

Sometimes it's difficult to know what's normal and what isn't. Many times during the grieving process, we will doubt our sanity. Although I don't know of any "Rules for Grief" carved in stone, there are some broad guidelines that may help.

It is normal to feel as if we were on the outside of ourselves watching all of this happening to someone else.

It is normal to feel a sense of disbelief, to say, "This can't be happening to me!" We feel as if life were suddenly a nightmare from which we cannot awaken.

It is normal to feel physically weak, light-headed, nauseated. We may be unable to sleep or to eat. We may feel nervous and unable to sit still—or exhausted and unable to move. We may need to sigh, yawn, or swallow and be completely unable to control it. Or we may have moments when we feel as if we were hyperventilating. Tears are totally beyond our conscious control. It is normal to feel as if we are going to faint. It is normal to need to hold on to others for actual physical support.

It is normal to feel a sense of panic and terror. We will, for a while, be unable to contemplate even the most immediate future without a feeling of helplessness. It is normal not to want to think of tomorrow.

It is normal to hear his car in the drive or his key in the lock. It's normal to hear her voice inside our head, to dream of her, to see her, just for a moment as we enter a room or drop off to sleep.

It is normal to want to cling to things that belonged to him, to sleep with his shirt, to hold his pillow. It is normal to smell her perfume, to read and reread the last "Honey-do" note she ever wrote.

When do such feelings become a cause for concern? That is hard to say. Because people are unique, they grieve in their own way and at their own speed. My eldest son postponed his grief by staying in the denial stage for much longer than the rest of us. After sixteen months he was just going through the resolving process that we'd tackled nearly a year before. He had held on to his pain longer than I, but was he still normal? Yes, he was.

Abnormality in grief is more a matter of degree than of content. One widow found that dinnertime was the hardest, so she made up a game of pretending that her husband was on a business trip and would be home tomorrow. After several months she realized that she was infusing her children with her fantasy, and she stopped doing it on her own. Another widow slept fully clothed on her couch for eighteen months following her husband's death because the empty bed was a symbol for her that he was truly gone. She finally realized that her grief was not progressing normally and sought grief counseling with a psychologist.

One thing that sometimes comes up at this point in the process is the question of medication. You know the Hollywood stereotype of grief: Someone is given a bit of shocking news, and the others immediately run for the brandy flask or the hypodermic needle. Beware! The message here is clear: No one should have to feel such pain; there should be instant relief and instant solutions.

Grief, like most truly real things in life, isn't subject to instant solutions. It is a process, and, like all processes that bring growth, it is painful. Dulling the pain with chemicals prevents us from moving through the process and resolving within ourselves what has happened. It numbs the feelings and dams the progress as surely as Hoover Dam blocks the Colorado River. And, like the waters of Lake Mead, the grief doesn't go away but builds up behind the dam. Sooner or later, even years later, it will burst forth, and the results are often devastating.

The day after I received the news of my husband's death, I was on my way to the lawyer's office with my sixteen-year-old son. In my son's words, I "freaked out." The only way I can describe the horror of that experience was that it washed pain over my body from my feet to my head in wave after wave of agony that I could not stop no matter how hard I tried. I flung my mind frantically in every direction, searching for something positive on which I could focus for survival. I found nothing. Later I was to equate that agony to labor pains during the transitional stage of labor when one pain does not peak and subside before the next one begins.

I became hysterical and wanted to scream and to run. My son, who was scared to death that I would bail out of the car on the freeway, drove me to the doctor's office, where they did sedate me. But that wise doctor gave me, along with the sedative, the message that the medication was a brief, stop-gap measure for an emergency situation only. He would not allow me to use the drug injudiciously to block out all feeling. In fact, when someone else tried to give me a tranquilizer the day of the funeral, I refused; somehow I knew that I needed to be alert and to feel all that was there for me to feel.

Contrast that with the woman whose doctor prescribed a strong tranquilizer for her following the death of her young son. In expressing his sympathy for her at the unfairness of a life that would deal her such a blow, the doctor sent her the unmistakable message that she should not have to cope with such pain. She bought the message and the drug therapy; a year later she was having to deal with severe Valium addiction—besides the unresolved grief.

One of the great ironies of grief is that it is during this first stage of intense shock that so many decisions must be made: funeral and burial arrangements must be attended to—a coffin chosen, a cemetery plot selected, and music, speakers, and flowers arranged for. Some decisions truly are major, such as choosing between burial or cremation. Money is an important concern. People's feelings are tenderly involved, so that even seemingly minor decisions like who rides with whom to the cemetery, assume major proportions.

If I could offer any practical advice, it would be to make only those decisions that absolutely have to be made at the time. In other words, up until the funeral, we should make only those decisions relating to the funeral, and not worry about the house or when we will go back to work or anything else. It was in allowing others to push me off to the lawyer's office prematurely that I was jolted out of shock and into hysteria. We need to live one day at a time—one hour at a time, if necessary.

We should delegate only those things we feel comfortable in delegating and accept the help of friends and neighbors who bring in meals or who want to mow the grass or sweep the floor. But if we feel the need to personally choose the coffin, we should do it. If we don't feel up to making that choice and we want help, then we should ask for it. The point is that *we* decide. We don't have to let someone else take over for us and make decisions for us that we want and need to make for ourselves. Only we know what we can and cannot do at the time.

Following the funeral a lot of our support is suddenly withdrawn. One widow observed that outside concern for her welfare wilted about the same time the flowers did. That is so true! Life seeks an equilibrium, a "return to normal." For those on the fringes, that happens shortly after the funeral. For those of us who are deeply involved, it takes much longer. Just when we need others the most, we may find ourselves more alone than ever. People seem to shun us as if widowhood were contagious. We're suddenly a threat, a single person in a married world. We're a reminder that the loved one is gone. We are a walking symbol of pain.

Many more decisions have to be made. Car titles and house deeds have to be transferred. Wills and other legal matters must be dealt with. Social security and life insurance and bank accounts and retirement funds—all of those things become a pressing reality at a time when just getting out of bed and brushing our teeth takes more energy than we've got.

I found that I needed expert advice at this point, and I consulted an attorney. In this way I retained ultimate control of the situation while being guided and protected at a time when I was most vulnerable. I also recommend consulting a good accountant for at least the first income-tax year after the death of a spouse. The law has many complexities regarding the financial aspects of an estate—complexities that we could easily miss even under the best of circumstances.

A final bit of practical advice that was given to me is to refrain from making any major decisions (such as moving, selling the house, and so on) for at least one full year. Time has borne witness to me of the soundness of that advice.

We make many necessary decisions while numb in our cocoon. In truth, shock serves a beneficial purpose. It's like a shot of emotional Novocain that keeps the full realization of the immensity of our loss in abeyance so that we can perform all of the necessary duties. I wept as I held my husband's hand at the viewing, but I sat dry-eyed through his funeral. It was shock that allowed me to bear my testimony the Sunday after the funeral. It was shock that gave a gallant widower the strength to stand at the pulpit after his wife's and baby's funeral to thank all those who had helped him. It is shock that somehow gets the meals on the table and the children dressed and the survivors back into the world. It is shock that lets us put one foot in front of the other until we have time to build within ourselves the real strengths that will get us through.

CHAPTER THREE

If Only . . .

I am troubled; I am bowed down greatly; I go mourning all the day long.

For mine iniquities are gone over mine head: as an heavy burden they are too heavy for me.

Deliver me from all my transgressions: make me not the reproach of the foolish. . . .

Hear my prayer, O Lord, and give ear unto my cry; hold not thy peace at my tears. . . . O spare me, that I may recover strength, before I go hence, and be no more.

Psalms 38:6, 4; 39:8, 12–13

August 29, 1982

I called sub service and got the recording. "My husband has been killed," I heard myself saying. "I'll need a sub at least until Wednesday."

Where was Carmon's sister? Why wasn't she here yet? Why wouldn't the clock move faster? Why couldn't my mom get here? Why couldn't Carm come home? I read the note on the refrigerator again and again: "Dear Kathy, Call the doctor Friday about my blood tests. See you Sunday. I love you, Carmy." It was Sunday. Where was he?

I forgot to call the doctor. I was so relieved when the doctor called me. I thought, "How lucky I am. I'll never have to tell Carmon that I got busy and forgot him." Now it doesn't much matter, but I still know: I got busy and forgot him.

Thursday when I left for work, I was in such a hurry that I didn't take time to kiss him good-bye. Then I went to lunch with Bonnie and Lisa, and I didn't even call home at noon to say good-bye.

And now he's never coming home again.

*G*uilt is very much a part of the grieving process. It's all of those terribly sad "if only's," "I should haves," and "Why didn't I's." The poet Whittier said, "Of all sad words of tongue or pen, / The saddest are these: 'It might have been.'"

There are times in every relationship when we are ill or tired or busy or just plain selfish, and we act less thoughtfully than we know we should. But what monumental proportions such small things assume when death intervenes with its great sense of finality and removes for us the opportunity to tell our loved one that we are truly sorry. Somehow death seems to negate for us the right to be human.

A story was told to me of an elderly widow who had spent the last years of her husband's life literally waiting on his every need. She had been an active woman in her community, sung in the choir at church, attended the Wednesday evening potlucks, lived a full and busy life. Then her beloved husband—let's call him Tom—fell ill and became almost bedridden. This lovely woman put her whole energy into caring for him while her own life went willingly onto the back burner.

On one such day, Tom had been particularly peevish and restless. She found herself going up and down the stairs, running countless errands, until by bedtime she was totally exhausted, both mentally and physically. She had just collapsed into her bed when she heard Tom calling, "I'm thirsty. Get me a drink of water."

She thought about those awful stairs and about her tired body, and she answered back, "Oh, go to sleep, Tom! I'll get you a drink in the morning."

Tom died that night.

What do you think this woman remembers? Does she take comfort in the memory of her two years of selfless service? Does she recall nearly sixty years of devotion in her marriage? No. What glares out of her memory are only those last few words, "Oh, go to sleep, Tom! I'll get you a drink in the morning."

So many things make us feel guilty. Often, people who are

in the numb state of shock and denial feel guilty because they "feel nothing" or because they cannot cry. Such people need to know that the numbness is part of the grieving process and is normal. Dry eyes or wet eyes are not the mark of the degree of love one feels for the deceased. Mourners may feel guilty for the anger they feel—anger at the deceased and anger at God.

Sometimes we feel guilty for the small things: the unspoken "I love you" or "I'm sorry"; the little kiss not given, the little service not performed. Other times the guilts are big— harsh, angry words or pain purposely inflicted—and the weight of the guilt seems a burden too heavy to bear. We become angry at ourselves and go over and over in our own mind what we did or did not do in relation to our loved one.

Guilt takes on a particularly somber tone when it relates—or seems to relate—to the circumstances surrounding the actual death. Tom's life would not have been extended by his having had that last drink of water, but it would be hard to convince his widow of that. And what of the husband who was driving the car when his wife was killed? Or the wife who waited too long to call the paramedics? Guilt can be:

"I should have taken him to another doctor."

"Why did I let her go alone?"

"I should never have left his bedside."

"Where was I when she needed me?"

"If only I'd insisted that he wear his seat belt."

"If I hadn't called her, she wouldn't have been out in the car."

"I was angry, sure, but I never wanted this to happen!"

Guilt. We rehearse it in our minds. We wear it as a mental hair shirt. We beat ourselves about the head with it. Seemingly there is nothing culturally acceptable we can do with this anger turned inward. We have no recourse to donning sackcloth and ashes as in biblical times. Yet we must do *something*. How, then, do we cope with such guilt?

First we need to know that guilt is to the spirit what pain is to the body. It is a signal to us that something is wrong, and it must signal to us strongly enough to motivate us to do something about it so that we can help ourselves begin to heal. Guilt lets us know that our real self is out of line with our ideal self. This lack of harmony needs to be rectified in order for healing to take place. But all too often we allow our guilt to go beyond what is necessary, beyond that signaling function.

When you were a child, did you ever have a sore on your body that you just couldn't leave alone? You picked and you scratched until the scab came off and the sore began bleeding and maybe even became infected. We do the same thing with our guilt, mistakenly telling ourselves that in doing so, we are keeping ourselves humble. In reality, though, what we accomplish is keeping our souls open and bleeding, in which condition they cannot heal or grow.

It seems easy to say, "Don't listen to the 'If only's'—they are irrational." But when we grieve, we are seldom rational. In fact, it isn't important whether our feelings of guilt seem rational or irrational to anyone else. If concerns or guilt are causing *us* pain, then they need to be dealt with following the same steps one would use in dealing with any other guilty feeling. *I* might know that my husband's death was not a result of my eight-year-old son's falling asleep in front of the TV that Saturday night and forgetting to say his prayers and ask for Heavenly Father to watch over his dad. I might even tell my son that a kind Heavenly Father wouldn't punish a sleepy little boy by taking his daddy away. But until that little boy poured out his heart to his Heavenly Father and felt that peaceful assurance for himself, it didn't matter much what *I* knew to be reasonable; it did matter what *my child* knew to be reasonable. His fears were a worry to *him;* they were important whether they were rational or not.

The first step in handling guilt is to recognize the problem realistically. Did we or did we not do something wrong? When a thought begins with "If only," we need to ask ourselves if we did the best we could have done, given the knowledge we had at that particular moment. If we did, then we may never need to go beyond this step. We may decide that we did not do anything wrong, and we can let the guilt go. If we decide we did do something we feel was wrong and we feel remorseful about it, we can move to the next step.

After recognition comes confession. Many mourners have found that talking to the deceased is very therapeutic. My eldest son spent many hours at his father's grave talking through some of their differences—differences that had been a part of the normal quest for independence of a young man growing up, but differences that caused my son concern nonetheless.

We don't need to go to the cemetery. We can put an empty chair in front of us and talk to the person, or talk to him or her while driving in our car, or anywhere that we are alone.

When we've talked to the deceased, we have, in essence, already confessed and expressed sorrow to him or her. But it's important for most of us to go beyond that. I love the twelve steps of sobriety espoused by members of Alcoholics Anonymous and find in them a practical guide for self-improvement that is applicable to many of life's situations when we find ourselves truly out of control. Since there are few, if any, situations more out of our control than the death of a loved one, I'd like to paraphrase a few of those steps as they can apply to grief.

One is to recognize that there are some aspects of our life that are beyond our control. We must be willing to turn those problems over to the Lord. We must make a restitution, whenever possible, to those whom we have hurt—when such restitution will not cause them further hurt. We must be willing to make amends to everyone involved, even though we might not be in a position to actually make such amends. We must confess our shortcomings to ourselves, to God, and to one other living person; we then can move forward with our lives, taking frequent inventory of our progress and seeking only to know God's will for us and praying for strength to do His will.

So after we've talked to the deceased, we can talk to our Heavenly Father. We have nothing to hide from Him anyway. Then we need to talk to "one other living person" in whom we have confidence. This may be a spiritual leader or simply a very close and trusted friend. We decide who it needs to be and choose someone who will listen empathetically in a way that will help us to grow.

After recognizing and confessing our shortcomings comes the step of making restitution. Here's where the bereaved hit a very big snag. How do we make restitution to a person who is dead and gone?

A therapeutic choice is to try to make a difference in someone else's life. If we're concerned because we didn't do something for the deceased that we feel we should have done, we must know that even if that person is beyond needing it, others are not; we can do it for someone else. One of my favorite stories of repentance is that of Ebenezer Scrooge. He couldn't repay old Fezziwig's kindness, but he could recompense by showing increased kindness to Bob Cratchit. He couldn't undo his selfishness to his young sweetheart, but he could be generous to Tiny Tim.

I think it helps to remember that the growth that will

come through this process is for us, not for the deceased. If we have increased in spiritual stature and have overcome some weakness as a result, then we have a repentant heart. A truly repentant heart is known to the Lord—and, I am confident, to our loved one who is gone. If we can forsake the shortcoming, we can let go of the "if only."

CHAPTER FOUR

Why Me?

My soul is weary of my life; I will leave my complaint upon myself; I will speak in the bitterness of my soul. I will say unto God, Do not condemn me; shew me wherefore thou contendest with me. Is it good unto thee that thou shouldest oppress, that thou shouldest despise the work of thine hands, and shine upon the counsel of the wicked?

If I sin, then thou markest me, and thou wilt not acquit me from mine iniquity. If I be wicked, woe unto me; and if I be righteous, yet will I not lift up my head. I am full of confusion; therefore see thou mine affliction; for it increaseth.

Job 10:1–3, 14–16

NOVEMBER 16, 1982

Yesterday would have been Carmon's forty-third birthday. Needless to say, it was a very difficult day for me. I awoke with the same empty pit of loneliness inside that I feel most mornings. It would be nice to wake up full of joy and anticipation. It's been so long that I've forgotten what joy feels like. Sometimes the pain is almost more than I can bear.

Why did God let this happen to us? It took us seventeen of our twenty years of marriage to get to that beautiful oneness. Just when we felt that comfortable "best friend" closeness, it was snatched away from me!

Tonight I went with Christy to a "Know Your Religion" lecture. It was really a beautiful meeting. I wish I could maintain such a spiritual level of feeling. I especially liked a quote from Boyd K. Packer when he said, "I'm delighted to hear that the adversary is upset. Monumental things must be about to happen." Well, monumental things must be about to happen for me and my family, for the adversary has been on my coattails ever since Carmon died. Everything that can break has: the washer, the dryer, both cars, the dishwasher, the sump pump; the septic tank backed up and the water lines broke, and I have to replace the kitchen floor where the washer leaked, and clean the carpets where the sump pump backed up.

Sometimes I get so mad at Carmon for leaving me with all this mess. Then I find myself pounding my fists on the wall again and again and demanding of the Lord, "How could you do this to me?!!" Some days I literally scream it.

I wonder if He will ever forgive me?

*F*eelings of anger were the hardest of all the emotions of grief for me to cope with. Because we are so emotionally vulnerable, it seems as though everything and everyone makes us angry when we mourn. I think it is because we feel so helpless. It's frustrating to have no control over such a major part of our life, and frustration is the close sibling of anger. Once hurt, our emotions are so tender that it's easy to keep bruising them on everything—like a sore thumb that keeps getting in the way. Every teeny bump registers major pain.

We can be mad at anyone even remotely connected with the death—the hospital, the doctors, nurses, policemen, morticians, anyone. We're angry with our family and our friends because they don't know what we're feeling and they don't know how to help us to stop the pain. We bump our fury on the bureaucracy of death certificates and funerals, social security and wills, banks and taxes. People can't even die without mountains of red tape!

Anyone who still has a living spouse is likely to upset us at the most unexpected moments. We find ourselves resenting couples who are close friends because they are still a whole unit. Gray-haired people growing old together upset us because we will never have that opportunity. Total strangers can trigger that angry tension as we ask, "How dare that person be alive when my best friend is dead!"

We are angry even with our mate for leaving us. One widow I heard of went to the cemetery and screamed at her husband for "slipping his skin" and leaving her with six small children.

Hardest to handle of all is the a
us a pain so indescribably awful and
so undeserved.

If you were reared, as I was, to perce
you likely will feel very guilty about your a
unable to control it. Just like so many thing. ... lives
these days, our emotions are out of whack, out of proportion,
and out of our control.

Rest assured, this is normal.

One of the most helpful lessons I have learned as I've
processed my own grief is that emotions are intrinsically
neither good nor bad; they just *are*. It is utter foolishness to
suppose we can go through life without ever feeling anger or
any of the more unpleasant emotions. It's what we *do* with
those emotions that determines whether they will have negative or positive effects. Somewhere along the line, we
assume—erroneously so—that what happens to us *causes*
our happiness or unhappiness. This is not true. It is how we
perceive what has happened to us and how we act upon that

ᴜn that results in the emotional reaction we feel. We ᴄᴀnnot always control what happens to us, but we can most certainly control the way we react to what has happened.

I personally find that concept a very powerful and optimistic one. If we can apply it at its highest levels, we can actually short-circuit the anger before it gets started. As time goes on and our grief-coping skills improve, we may choose to aim for that level of control.

But unless and until that improvement in coping with grief occurs, what do we do? How do we cope when anger rises up and almost blinds us? Again, it's what we do with the emotion, not the emotion itself, that will determine our ability to move forward.

First, we need to let ourselves own our feelings. We must not pretend that we're not angry when we are. Next, we must decide what to do with the anger once we have admitted to owning it. Anger shouldn't be directed against others, of course. Those who seek revenge, who nurse old wounds, or who speak or act cruelly toward their neighbors are "in danger of the judgment" (see Matthew 5:22), for they risk harming not only their neighbor but also themselves.

Anger shouldn't be directed inward, either. Suppressed anger is damaging to us emotionally, physically, and spiritually. It can surface in the form of ulcers, high blood pressure, migraine headaches, or any number of other disorders.

I found some ways to vent anger that remove the immediate stress and at the same time are not harmful to me or to others.

Vigorous physical activity is a tremendous reducer of stress. We can run, walk briskly, jump rope, swim, play tennis or racquetball, punch a speed bag, or do calisthenics. My personal choice was an aerobics dance class twice a week and early morning walks before work. Fringe benefits include better digestion, less insomnia, and improved cardiovascular functioning, in addition to a trimmer, firmer figure.

Working with our hands also helps. A good, hard housecleaning session cleans my mental house as well as my physical house. So do yard work and marathon cooking sessions. One woman I know takes out her anger on bread dough and then takes a fresh, hot loaf of that well-kneaded bread to whoever it was that made her angry in the first place.

Some days you may feel like screaming. Do it. Go into your room, shut the door so you won't scare kids, neighbors, or pets, and really yell. Pound your pillow if you have to. Cry. Act out your anger without hurting others or yourself. Vent some steam. Then wash your face, stand up tall, and go out to face the world again.

A really effective coping mechanism is simply to tell someone we are angry and why, to talk out our feelings with someone we can trust to listen quietly without lecturing us about the goodness or badness of what we are experiencing. We can talk to our dead spouse, talk to our spiritual leader, talk to our Heavenly Father. If someone has made us angry, we can talk to that person about it. I found that my feelings were so touchy that most people who hurt them were not aware they had done so. One friend in particular had really rubbed me the wrong way on several occasions. When I finally got the courage to go to her about it, it was a beautiful spiritual experience for both of us.

Creative expression often helps. We might draw or paint a picture of our anger, compose a song, write a poem or a story, or record it in our journal. Putting a label on an emotion helps us to cope with it.

Because a lot of the anger related to bereavement comes from frustrating situations beyond our control, we can take another page from Alcoholics Anonymous: "Let go. Let God." We can't control the fact that our spouse is dead, but we can control how we react to that fact.

A dying person once moaned, "Why me?" Elizabeth Kubler-Ross, who was listening, answered, "Why not you?" I've often thought of that when tempted to ask, "Why me, Lord?" Why not me? Why should I be spared the pain—or the opportunity for growth? Life isn't always fair in the mortal sense, and if we seek for it to be, we will be discouraged. But it is always fair in an eternal sense.

CHAPTER FIVE

I Just Want to Die

If thou art called to pass through tribulation; . . . if thou be cast into the deep; if the billowing surge conspire against thee; if fierce winds become thine enemy; if the heavens gather blackness, and all the elements combine to hedge up the way; and above all, if the very jaws of hell shall gape open the mouth wide after thee, know thou, my son, that all these things shall give thee experience, and shall be for thy good. The Son of Man hath descended below them all. Art thou greater than he?

Doctrine and Covenants 122:5, 7–8

NOVEMBER 16, 1982

Sometimes it still feels so unreal to me. It just isn't possible that half of me could really be dead. It's like some horrible, monstrous joke someone is playing on me.

DECEMBER 5, 1982

I'm sitting here by the fire, wrapped in a quilt, watching the lights twinkle on the Christmas tree. The calendar says that it is December, less than three weeks until Christmas. It is cold and hazy out today. We've had a night or two of freezing weather. The world rolls on, the seasons change from summer to autumn and now winter. I watch it all with a certain amazement, for in my heart it is still August 29. It should be hot outside. It's Sunday again, and he's still not home. He left me a note. He said, "I'll see you Sunday," but he never came. He never came!

DECEMBER 11, 1982

Some days I'm almost angry that God has given me so much knowledge of the plan of salvation that I can't ever cheer myself up with thoughts of suicide. There is something very depressing in the knowledge that the only future joy you see for yourself is in your own death.

The most devastating of all the stages of the grieving process is depression. It totally immobilizes the mourner. Small daily tasks of living become seemingly insurmountable obstacles. Everything seems to be without hope. A sense of fatalism sets in. There is no desire to live.

I used to think that depression was the opposite of anger, the one being so passive, the other so active. I have since learned that depression is simply farther down on the same negative continuum. When our guilt or our anger becomes despair, when our life is seemingly way out of our control, when we feel frustrated and helpless and hopeless, we are depressed.

Depression is the most dangerous of the stages of grief. When we are depressed and we don't care whether we live or die, we often actually endanger ourselves because we fail to take otherwise normal precautions with our physical well-being.

Death rates for widowed people are significantly higher than for the nonwidowed. For widowers the most dangerous time is during the first six months alone; widows are most vulnerable during the second year of widowhood.

One widow came home from the mortuary viewing of her husband's body, told her sister that she was tired, went to bed, and never woke up.

Another very young widow was killed in an automobile accident just three months after her husband, a police officer, had been killed in the line of duty.

An elderly widower, despondent over the loss of his wife, sought to take his own life.

Fortunately, most widowed people are not among those grim statistics. Most of us not only survive our depression but grow as a result of having experienced it. But the growth does not come without a price.

Physical symptoms of depression include loss of appetite,

extreme and chronic fatigue, lethargy, insomnia, change in bowel and bladder habits and other bodily functions, nightmares, weight loss, lowered resistance to illness and infection, frequent physical illnesses, shaking and trembling, inability to focus thought, lack of direction, inability to relax or to sit still, inability to move, nausea, light-headedness, inability to focus eyes, greater frequency of accidental injury, body aches, lack of concern for physical appearance . . . I could go on and on.

Most depressing of all is that we can look into the past or at the present or toward the future and see absolutely nothing positive anywhere. A feeling of total hopelessness settles in.

I often envisioned myself as a drowning person in the middle of a lake of despair. All of my friends and family were standing around on the shore watching me with pain and pity in their eyes, but no one threw me a lifeline. It wasn't until much later that I understood why: no one knew how. But at the time it made me angry, and that was good. The anger got me moving again. It brought me up out of the depression. I realized that there wasn't a soul who could truly help me but me.

In my case, the pain of depression was so great that it sought its own resolution as a matter of my survival. Here are some mental gymnastics I learned to perform in the process.

One problem-solving technique of mine is that when I don't understand something, I take a class about it. I did just that. Six months after my husband's death, I enrolled in a class called "Death, Dying, and Bereavement" at a local community college. Not only did I learn a lot about what was happening to me, but I also began to emerge from the lethargic routine into which I had fallen. It wasn't easy for me, and many times I had to act as if I were enthusiastic when I really was not. On one occasion, a field trip to a mortuary, I was unable to force myself to attend. But that was all right, and for the most part, I soon found that acting "as if" was giving way to actual enthusiasm—a tentative and embryonic enthusiasm, but enthusiasm nonetheless.

When I would, by some serendipitous occurrence, find something even minutely positive in the future, I would cling to it as a drowning person clings to a life preserver. It didn't matter that it wasn't some massive, exuberant contemplation. Bereavement isn't a time for exuberance. If I found one tiny glimmer, I'd cling to it. People told me to live one day at a time. I'm here to tell you that in the beginning I lived one *hour* at a time. I felt I'd reached a peak experience when I could plan one whole day. We must all learn to live our lives in tiny bites and cling to the small things.

We need to take care of our physical health, even when we don't want to do so. Because depression numbs our concern for ourselves and because it brings with it so many physical symptoms, being depressed tends to become a vicious and self-perpetuating cycle. Because we feel depressed, we don't eat properly and we don't sleep well. We become run-down and tired, which depresses us further. So it goes, in a downward spiral. We can break the physical aspect of the cycle by establishing as regular a routine of meals, sleep, and exercise as we can muster. We can take our vitamins, get out in the fresh air, see the doctor about flu shots, and do whatever we have to do to take care of our physical health even when we don't want to. If we'll start taking care of our physical needs out of duty, soon we'll want to care for those needs again out of desire.

Along that same line, we can get ourselves going on our physical appearance again. In the beginning it may take more energy than we've got just to get out of bed and get our teeth brushed, but we must do it. I was fortunate in that I had to go right back to work just a few days after the funeral. I had to get dressed and fix my hair and put on a little make-up. At first it was a chore, but after a while I found that I did care about how I looked and how I felt.

Finding others who had trod this same path helped me considerably. It was good to talk to other people who knew how I felt. It was helpful also to read the experiences of others. I found myself reading a lot. It helped to read back through my journal to see that I was indeed moving forward, even though on a day-to-day basis I couldn't feel the progress.

As I began to develop some strengths, it was a marvelous experience to be able to reach out to help other people who were not as far along in the grief process as I was. Many times, when I'd find myself slipping back into the depression cycle, I'd pray to the Lord to be rescued, and he would send me someone else with problems greater than my own.

Finally, it has helped me enormously to allow myself to be human. In the beginning I felt that I had to put up this brave front, to be the tower of strength for everyone. I pictured myself in a display case with the whole world looking to me as the perfect example of Mormon widowhood. To tell you the truth, I resented it. When I did get angry, I'd feel guilty, then depressed, then angry again. When did I get to be less than perfect? When did I get to scream and cry without shame? The answer was simple: when I allowed myself to do so; when I learned to accept myself as a person in process and not a finished product.

I remember several years ago listening to our stake patriarch speak on perfection. As I recalled his words, I began to see perfection in a new light—as a star by which to navigate the seas of our mortal existence, realizing full well that we'll never reach that star in this life. That wise man compared these two scriptures, words of the Savior: "Be ye therefore perfect, even as your Father which is in heaven is perfect" (Matthew 5:48), and "Therefore I would that ye should be perfect *even as I,* or your Father who is in heaven is perfect" (3 Nephi 12:48; italics added).

The first was spoken to the Jews, the second to the Nephites following Christ's resurrection. The patriarch told us that the difference in wording was not an error in translation; it was, in fact, a lesson to us that even the Savior, the world's most perfect person, did not call himself perfect until He had passed through all things, including temptation, despair, pain, death, and resurrection. As He told the Prophet Joseph Smith, "The Son of Man hath descended below them all. Art thou greater than he?" (D&C 122:8.)

CHAPTER SIX

Tomorrow I Will . . .

Fear not; for thou shalt not be ashamed: neither be thou confounded; for thou shalt not be put to shame: for thou shalt forget the shame of thy youth, and shalt not remember the reproach of thy widowhood any more.

For thy Maker is thine husband; the Lord of hosts is his name; and thy Redeemer the Holy One of Israel; The God of the whole earth shall he be called. For the Lord hath called thee as a woman forsaken and grieved in spirit, and a wife of youth, when thou wast refused, saith thy God.

For a small moment have I forsaken thee; but with great mercies will I gather thee. In a little wrath I hid my face from thee for a moment: but with everlasting kindness will I have mercy on thee, saith the Lord thy Redeemer. . . .

O thou afflicted, tossed with tempest, and not comforted, behold, I will lay thy stones with fair colours, and lay thy foundations with sapphires. And I will make thy windows of agates, and thy gates of carbuncles, and all thy borders of pleasant stones. And all thy children shall be taught of the Lord; and great shall be the peace of thy children.

Isaiah 54:4–8, 11–13

MARCH 27, 1983

Next week is Easter. Shawn is in the Mesa Temple pageant this year, playing the part of a Roman soldier. It has kept him extra busy and I have missed his comfort and companionship. I've also missed his help with errands. I give him a lot of responsibility, and I rely on him heavily.

You know, it's interesting when I look at the kids. They've grown so much these past months. It is especially noticeable with Shawn. If his physical stature matched his spiritual stature we'd have to knock out our ceilings because he'd be ten feet tall.

I've been reading a book by Catherine Marshall called Meeting God at Every Turn *in which she points out chapter 54 of Isaiah as "must" reading for widows. I read it and found great comfort there, even though I know he was talking to Israel and not to an individual. I especially like the part that promises that "all thy children shall be taught of the Lord." I can look at mine and see that that is true. Some days when I feel as though I'm going nowhere with my grief, I'll look at them and know in my heart that I am.*

Oh, I had an interesting experience last week. I had to pick up a little girl from my class at school, so I was driving a different route to work. I was passing the orange groves on North Higley Road, lost as usual in my gloom, when I suddenly became aware of the sweetest fragrance. It startled me as it dawned on me that I was smelling orange blossoms. As I slowed down to drink it in, I noticed how green the leaves were and how I could hear birds singing in the trees. A roadrunner skirted the edge of the grove and disappeared in the soft grass. The most peaceful feeling settled in my breast, and my eyes welled up with tears. The trees had been blossoming for many days; I'd just never noticed them before.

I remember the indescribable pain the first time I went to the temple alone just a few weeks after my husband's death. There are no words to convey the emptiness I felt as I entered the celestial room and he was not there. Waves of grief washed over my soul until I thought I could bear it no longer. I sat with tears streaming down my face and pleaded with the Lord to take away my pain, even if to do so meant taking my life. Then the Spirit whispered to me in quiet but unmistakable tones, "Not yet, my daughter. This is something you must bear for a small season."

When we grieve, it is so painful that we invest every ounce of our emotional energy in coping with that pain. We live an absolutely survival level of existence. That is why grief is so exhausting—emotionally, mentally, spiritually, and physically. Grief truly drains all of our reserves.

Our focus is on the past, on real memories and on fantasies of "what might have been." We go over and over in our minds what has happened. We "rewrite" the ending more to our liking. Even our dreams have a haunted quality as they replay the circumstances surrounding the death. We feel deserted and betrayed.

We begin to reckon time as "before the death" and "after the death." Things become marked for their antiquity when they are labeled as having occurred "when Daddy was still alive." It seems as if the death was only yesterday and a million years ago, all at the same time. It's hard to remember not being alone.

As we work through the anger and the guilt and the depression, some days it seems as if we're spinning our emotional wheels and going nowhere. Life becomes a manic-depressive roller-coaster ride; we're afraid to allow ourselves to feel good, because we know that feeling good is always followed by a plunge into the pit of despair.

People tell us that time heals all wounds; but as the months pass by, we begin to wonder *when?* How much time does it take for the healing to begin?

One mistake I made was in looking for things to be normal again, and I equated *normal* with *same.* Things can never be the same again, nor would we want them to be. Waters that never move become stagnant, and so do people. But things can be normal again if we can grow to the point where we redefine *normal* to mean "normal under *new* circumstances."

Another mistake I made was in expecting it would happen in one fell swoop. After all, the pain came in an instant; why couldn't it go away in an instant? It was that kind of expectation that left me devastated every time I'd get a small glimmer of happiness only to find that it didn't last forever.

Like all of the truly meaningful experiences in life, grief is resolved in the small moments, the tiny touches of revealed truth, the almost imperceptible lifts of emotions.

For weeks and months we've been investing all of our energy in dealing with the pain of grieving and in coming to terms with the past. We can't put all of that away in one moment and force ourselves to look only toward the future. Resolution of grief is not something that can be overtly controlled; rather, it must be dealt with on a feeling level as well as a thinking level over an extended period of time.

Resolving grief is more than just accepting the death. It involves gradually reinvesting that emotional energy, not in the past, but in the future; not in pain, but in growth.

In the beginning, it's very tentative. I like to picture it as a small child dipping one toe into the cold water of a pool. It may take many gradual dips before he risks getting all wet. Some people may be able to plunge in head first, but the shock to the system is such that, with grief at least, dipping is better.

As we begin to shift all that tremendous energy from the past, we must refocus our sights and place that energy into something in our new and future life. Resolving grief, in fact, involves the almost total restructuring of one's life.

Resolution comes in the tiny moments: the first time we realize that we've done a whole week's marketing all alone; the first time we hear "that song" and know that the tears are sweet and not bitter; the first time we smell a flower again or see sunshine and color and are truly aware of those sensations. Resolution is the first Sunday that passes and we're suddenly aware that it *has* passed without significance. Resolution is when our picky, foot-in-her-mouth friend says something personal and we're not offended. Resolution is when we reread the obituary and realize that "survivor" really means us. Resolution is when we find ourselves think-ing about tomorrow.

How long does it take? That depends on each of us and our individual makeup. We can't force it, but we can under-stand the process. Knowing what to expect, knowing that we are normal, makes it easier to bear. We can give ourselves permission to grieve and not try to fight it; that in itself will expedite the process. I learned through painful experience that every time I tried to force the process or to deny it, I was devastated. I've always been one to say, "Give me patience, Lord, and hurry!" But grief has taught me to go with the flow and to say, "Not my will, but thine."

Experts say that the first six to eighteen months are the hardest. There is a desperate yearning for the loved one and a search for some meaning. It helped me to know that in this life, at least, there are some questions for which there are no answers. I like this line from Maria Von Trapp's book *The Trapp Family Singers:* "God's will hath no why." It helped me to wait out the healing time.

Although there are no magical numbers, most widowed people I've talked to feel that the first year is the significant time. During that year we so often find ourselves saying or thinking, "Last year at this time we were ..." After the first anniversary of the death, we no longer need to do that. All those difficult firsts are past: the first Christmas alone, the first birthday, the first anniversary. I remember looking forward to that milestone with a mixture of anticipation and anxiety. It was like contemplating the birth of a child. There was anxiety in the knowledge that there would be pain but anticipation in knowing that following the pain would come a new and beautiful life. It was like a new birth to me. I felt that the burden of centuries was lifted from my shoulders, that I could take my life off "hold" and move forward again.

A short time later I was in the temple again. This time I found myself drinking in the peace and beauty that was there. Again I sat in the celestial room, and the Spirit whispered to my soul, "The season is passing."

CHAPTER SEVEN

A Time to Mourn

To every thing there is a season, and a time to every purpose under the heaven: A time to be born, and a time to die; a time to plant, and a time to pluck up that which is planted; a time to kill, and a time to heal; a time to break down, and a time to build up; a time to weep, and a time to laugh; a time to mourn, and a time to dance.

Ecclesiastes 3:1–4

January 15, 1983

Lynne called today. She thinks I've been mourning long enough, so she's coming to pick me up tonight and we're going to a dance.

January 16, 1983

Never again! I've never had such a degrading experience. I felt like a piece of meat on the butcher's shelf. Men were talking to me in such a condescending manner, treating me like I was thirteen years old and without a brain in my head!

I went to a fireside tonight and it wasn't any better. The speaker was good, but afterward, during the refreshments, it was ridiculous. Everyone was milling around like some kind of lonely hearts club. The women looked desperate and frustrated, and the men acted like kids in a candy store. One man came up to me and told me that if I'd start coming to the singles' dances he'd save a dance or two. To top it off, it looked like he hadn't shaved since work on Friday.

I told my kids that if the Lord wants me to marry again,

He's going to have to bring someone to my doorstep. I'm one of the great women of the world! I don't have to put up with that!

In Ecclesiastes we read that there is a time to mourn and a time to dance. When we let others decide our time frame for us, we may be setting ourselves up for being pushed into something for which we are not ready. That particular January I was still in mourning; I was angry and depressed; I was months away from resolution. If I had listened to my own feelings, I would have known that it wasn't my time to dance.

Knowing our own heart and following it is one of the practical coping skills we develop as grieving progresses. To truly resolve our grief over the loss, we must learn to stand alone and to make our own decisions—and to accept totally the consequences for those choices.

People grieve for many things besides the loss of a loved one. They grieve for the loss of a lifestyle or personal identity; loss of home, employment, or financial status; loss of health or sexual function. When we suddenly find ourselves single persons in a married world, we grieve for most of those things all at once. Even after we've said good-bye and finally buried our dead, we still cope with the gamut of adjustments involved in sudden singleness.

Part of the enormous anger I had to overcome was due to that adjustment from being married to being single. I felt that I had worked very hard at my marriage. Of course I loved my husband, but I also had hung in there through all the tough times because I never wanted to be alone; I never wanted to be a single parent; I never wanted to raise my children in what I considered to be half a home. So I took my marriage covenants very literally and worked hard during those years of adjustment. Then, just when life was getting comfortable, just when the children were beyond the diapers and bottles stage, just when things were coming together financially, just when we finally achieved that best-friend, one-flesh relationship—*bam!* He was dead, and in an instant I was alone anyway. I was a single parent, and my children were in a fatherless home. I could scarcely contain my fury for months. Even when I had quite resolved my grief over Carmon's death, I was dealing daily with the trial of single-ness, a type of grief all its own.

Now, I wouldn't be presumptuous enough to propose that only single people have problems. Having been both married and single, I know that marriage can be the best of times or the worst of times. I also know that in a nurturing marriage the problems seem half as bad and the happiness twice as good. Single people don't have that one intimate other to share both joy and pain. They must develop other support systems. Those who become "suddenly single" of necessity face a total restructuring of their lives.

I also wouldn't be presumptuous enough to suppose that I have any definitive answers to that quest for a new struc-ture. All I can offer are some admittedly personal insights that I have gleaned during my struggles—with the confes-sion that I am still struggling.

One thing I have learned through my mistakes is to get to

know myself, to know who, what, and where I am. I have had to discover my own time frame for adjustment and to refuse to allow others, no matter how well-meaning they may be, to push me into situations for which I am not ready. We all have to mourn when we should mourn, and dance when we should dance.

Another thing I have had to learn and relearn is that attitude is the deciding factor in any aspect of life. When I first became single, I was horrified at the frustration and desperation I saw all around me. I saw single people buying the stigma that they were somehow second-class citizens because they had failed, for whatever reason, to measure up to some narrowly defined, stereotypical image of what people should be. In the beginning I clung to my "great woman of the world" self-image fairly well; but in so doing, I failed to appreciate many of my new single associates. Then I began to feel rejected; I began to notice married friends dropping away because I no longer belonged. Pretty soon I began to feel frustrated and desperate. My self-image was shattered, and I began to feel that I deserved to be pitied or degraded.

Then one day, as I was preparing to speak to a group of single people about grief, I took a good look at myself and said, "Hey, wait a minute! I am a child of God, and I have value just because I exist. It doesn't matter what my marital status is—I have a lot to offer this world. My children are fed and clothed and housed; they are taught honesty and integrity, and above all else, they are loved dearly. There is nothing 'broken' about our home just because circumstance has decreed that a father's physical presence is no longer there. I am not a second-class anybody, and neither are any of my single brothers and sisters. We are all children of God!"

In that moment, I realized that I had been buying into the stereotype, too, by pigeonholing both myself and other single people. When I changed my attitude, I came to appreciate myself again and to appreciate many new and wonderful friends. A few months ago I saw the man from my first fireside singing in a church choir of singles. As I watched the emotion with which he poured his heart into that hymn, I realized that it didn't matter how often he shaved.

If we have a stigma of "single is second best," it's not because someone has put it there but because we have taken it upon ourselves. Others may try to thrust it on us with their poor attitudes, but we don't have to buy it.

A final thing that I have learned is so plain that it sounds simplistic. In fact, I hesitate to mention it for fear of sounding like Pollyanna, but it works for me, so I will. There is a line in one of our hymns that reads, "By strict obedience Jesus won . . . " How startled I was when it hit me one day that nothing in this life is "won" by any other means. If we are having a problem and we need help, then we need to obey the law upon which that help is predicated. (See D&C 130:20–21.) In other words, we must live as closely as we possibly can to what we know to be right. It's when our behavior gets out of line with our ideals that we get into emotional deep water.

To give you some practical examples of what I mean, let's

look at a common problem for single people: money. When Carmon died, it took about three months before we could collect any life insurance or social security benefits. Until then, we had to get by on what I made teaching school— which was about one-third of our usual income. It would have been tempting to say, "I can't afford to pay tithing right now." But I was alone and afraid. I took the position that I couldn't afford *not* to pay tithing; I needed those windows of heaven open! I could give example after example of the literal fulfillment of that promise. One week both of my cars broke down and needed parts; that very day my principal showed up with an envelope of money my colleagues had collected in my behalf. Another time we needed groceries, and a check arrived from the members of my parents' ward in another state. Once I was feeling blue and wishing I could take the kids out for a hamburger just to get away from the house for a while. That was a luxury, not even a necessity; and yet, when I opened the mail that day, there was a check from a family that had known me as a child. From those and other experiences, I came to regard tithing not as a demand but as a privilege.

Another law that should be approached as a "thou shalt" instead of as a "thou shalt not" is the law of chastity. It was very difficult for me, having been married for twenty years, to suddenly find myself in a position of no longer having that special intimacy with a person I loved. I knew that I wanted to stay chaste, but as long as I looked at the law with an attitude of self-denial, it made me angry. I obeyed, but out of a sense of duty. It all seemed so unfair.

Then, almost imperceptibly, my attitude began to change. As I continued to apply God's laws in my relationships with other people, I began to sense a tremendous strength and power in chastity. I became fascinated with the idea that the Lord's rules for physical intimacy are given to us not to deny us pleasures of the flesh but to protect us. We have the assurance that if we follow his guidelines, we will experience physical intimacy only where there is an equally strong emotional intimacy and under the protection of a long-term commitment.

Understanding chastity as a positive force, as a gift from God, and not as a "No," dissolved a lot of anger for me.

It is still difficult to deal with the temptations. The feelings and desires are there. In the beginning there were no feelings because, like other physical appetites, they were silenced by the intensity of the grief. But rest assured, they do return, and I have come to realize that it is a positive and healthy sign when they do. They indicate that we are healing and looking forward again. We just have to make sure that we recognize in those desires the righteous goals for which our Heavenly Father gave them to us.

Yes, I want to love again. I think most of us do. The need to love and to be loved in return is basic to all of us. That is a righteous goal that fuels our desires. It's a shame that in English we have only one word for love; it's a bigger shame that we often misuse that one. The Greeks have several words for love. One of those is *eros,* from which comes our English word *erotic.* I've felt great sorrow that we so often narrowly define love only as *eros.* The love that we need to truly fill

those desires we feel is *agape,* the love that is defined in First
Corinthians, chapter 13: love that is kind, patient, not envi-
ous, not self-seeking, but giving and sharing, and most of
all, unconditional. *Eros* is part of that love between a man
and a woman, but only a part. In the gestalt of love, the
whole is much greater than the sum of its parts.

I said earlier that we grieve for many things. As we adjust
to our situation, we move from an attitude of loss to an attitude of growth. One of the many things that helped me to
move in that direction was a widow's support group called
THEOS. With their permission, I'd like to share their
"Challenges to the Widowed":

1. Try to recognize death as another step in God's plan for
the full development of a person and to accept the life-death
cycle as common to all creation.

2. Strive, as a person coming to understand yourself, to
learn about and understand the normal cycle of grief.

3. Allow yourself sufficient time to let the grieving take its

natural course and insist that others allow you this time as well.

4. Try to come to a full discovery of yourself as an individual, as a complete person capable of looking to your own needs and desires and of controlling and coming to grips with your emotions.

5. Work to overcome boredom and self-pity, to break the old twenty-four hours routine, even to accept solitude, while pushing out to the new interests and accepting the help of others as you come to recognize your own individual self-worth and self-esteem.

6. Do not live through your children but continue to love them and care for them very much so that you can draw strength from one another.

7. Learn to make your own decisions with confidence and faith rather than looking for a replacement or substitute to make them for you.

8. Learn to accept people as they are, not as you would like them to be.

9. Forget about becoming your "old self" again. Renewed

faith in God and in yourself will make you an even better person, capable of both loving and living normally again.

10. Assist others, especially your children, in preparing for possible widowhood themselves by instructing them in wills and finances, in the importance of sharing decisions in marriage, in the dangers of overdependence on one's spouse, and about the advantages of involvement in community and church affairs.

11. Help to educate the "couples-oriented" society to an understanding of widowhood and the distinct contribution of widowed persons to church, government, and community interests and to the worlds of business, health care, and education.

12. As one who has come through the grief of widowhood, share your strength, faith, hope, and experience with others who are still struggling with their grief.

CHAPTER EIGHT

Suffer the Little Children

Then were there brought unto him little children, that he should put his hands on them, and pray: and the disciples rebuked them. But Jesus said, Suffer little children, and forbid them not, to come unto me: for of such is the kingdom of heaven.

Matthew 19:13–14

Fall 1982

Terri was really gloomy today. She just sat on the couch and stared off into space. When I asked her what was wrong, at first she wouldn't answer. So I sat quietly and listened. Finally she said she was thinking of her dad and of the last time we went camping. "I was mad at him, Mom, and I told him that I hated him."

"And that makes you feel guilty?" I said it so quietly that I wasn't sure she'd heard me until I saw the tears well up in her eyes and her head slowly nodding. "Yes."

Spring 1983

Shawn came into my bedroom last night after his date. He always checks in when he gets home. He seemed really pensive, though, last night. He said to me, "Mom, sometimes I almost wish you had died and not Dad."

"Why?" I asked.

"Because if you had died, your folks would have said, 'With Kath gone, the kids will need us more than ever.' We never see

Dad's family. Sometimes I think they don't think we belong to them anymore."

WINTER 1983

I had a big hassle with Terri the other day, and Shane started to cry. I tried to send him from the room—told him it wasn't his problem—but he wouldn't go. He just stuck out that defiant little chin of his and said, "No, I'm not leaving you, Mom."

When Terri finally went into the other room, Shane ran into my arms and dissolved in tears. "Why, what on earth is the matter?" I asked him.

Through his heaving sobs he finally whispered, "I was so scared, Mom. I'm afraid sometimes. I'm afraid I'm going to lose you too."

Children are the forgotten mourners. Like us, they go through shock, anger, guilt, and depression. Like us, given time, they work through their grief to resolution. Unfortunately, we often don't allow children to own their feelings. We send all sorts of verbal and nonverbal messages that "big boys mustn't cry" or "good little girls shouldn't get angry." That makes the whole grieving process frightening and confusing to them.

When a parent dies, a child's worst nightmares become reality. We, the surviving parent, have to help our children make that nightmare bearable at a time when we are ill-equipped to handle our own pain.

Fortunately, society is starting to move away from the idea that we need to protect children from death. We just need to work through our own feelings about it so that we can handle grief realistically and honestly with our children.

I was glad that in our home we had been working for a long time to establish an open sharing of feelings. The atmosphere we had been able to achieve helped immensely as the children and I gingerly picked our way through our own grief. My children felt safe in sharing their feelings; that, I am sure, accounts for the outstanding job they have done with their grief work.

There are certain responses to death that, if not unique to children, are at least more obvious in children. I noticed them in my own three, who were eight, twelve, and sixteen at the time of their father's death. I even noticed them to a certain extent in my oldest son, who at nineteen was married and no longer living at home.

Children worry about what happens to the physical body. They need to have explained to them simply and plainly what is to be done with the remains. My eldest, Brian, even went so far as to work as an apprentice in a mortuary for almost a year following his father's death. It was part of the processing he felt he had to do. It gave him a sense of control over the physical aspect of death.

Young people also worry when the memories begin to fade. I remember Shawn's consternation the first time he realized he could no longer remember the sound of his dad's voice. Children need to be reassured that fading memory is normal and healthy and that it in no way means they didn't love the parent enough.

Children have a lot of fear relating to the death. If some well-meaning person tells a small child that the dead person "was so good that God took him up to heaven," then the child may be afraid to be good. If a person tells the child, "He just got sick and died," the child may be terrified by illness. I remember my husband telling me how he was afraid he'd die when he had his appendix removed as a youngster. His father had died of appendicitis.

A child may feel afraid to love because "I loved Daddy and he died. If I love Mommy, will she die too?" A few weeks after Carmon's death, someone poisoned Shane's dog. I'll never forget his bitter tears as he said over and over again, "Everything I love dies; everything I love dies."

The child may be afraid to be alone. He may be afraid to ride in a car if the parent died in an accident. He may be afraid to go to the doctor or to a hospital if the parent died of an illness.

The child may fear that the remaining parent will die, leaving the child all alone. In the early days of my grief, the pressure of rearing three children by myself was about to drive me crazy. My mother, thinking to secure the children's cooperation for me, told my daughter that she'd better be good because if I had a nervous breakdown, Grandma was not going to take care of her (although I know she would have). It was quite a while before it dawned on me what Terri's problem was. When I finally realized the burden she was carrying, I reassured her and her brothers that I probably would not have a nervous breakdown or die; but even if I did, I had made legal provisions for their grandparents to care for them. They all needed to know that they would not be left alone.

Children often get very angry with the living parent. After all, that parent is going through a rough time himself or herself and is no peach to live with. Also, with only one parent calling the shots, there is no court of appeals or mediation within the family to which the child can turn. A child can feel very helpless in that situation.

The child may wish the living parent had died instead

and may even say so. Both parent and child need to know that such feelings are normal. When we remember the dead person, we tend to remember only the good things, especially at first. We forget that he or she was cranky and unreasonable at times too. The flesh-and-blood survivor who is still blundering through this existence might come up awfully short by comparison.

Children are very upset by the way we grown-ups behave. They need to be told honestly that we too are grieving, that right now we're angry and upset and confused, but that it won't last forever. They need important grown-ups in their lives. They need strong reassurances of a sense of family and belonging. It was hard for my children to understand that their father's relatives were grieving too and that to be around our home was difficult for them. How wonderful it was when those sweet sisters-in-law and brothers-in-law would call or come, thus reassuring my children that they were still a part of the clan.

The child might feel guilty and think that he or she

caused the death. All children at one time or another experience anger with a parent. They may say "I hate you." They may even wish that the offending parent would, in fact, die. When that parent does die, the burden of guilt on the child can be tremendous. I have always appreciated Fred Rogers of "Mr. Rogers' Neighborhood," who tells children that "angry, mad wishes don't make things come true." It is a concept I borrow and use when I work with children in this situation.

Children feel confused because grown-ups tell them how they should feel and what they should do. They may even get mixed messages, with one person telling them, "Now, I want you to be brave and not cry," while another adult counsels, "Cry, you'll feel better." I tried to be open with my kids about my feelings and their feelings. It helped me to clarify some of the mixed messages they were receiving elsewhere.

Children, like a lot of grown-ups, want things to change quickly. When a parent dies, they may want the remaining parent to remarry right away. It may even confuse them that they want that to happen while at the same time they are missing the deceased parent. It helps to tell them that they are normal. A lot of grown-ups feel the same mixture of feelings when they have been widowed. We were all happy once, and we want to be happy again. There is nothing wrong with that. I'll never forget Shane's coming home from school one day, just a few weeks after Carmon's death. He was mad at the world. When I asked him what was wrong, he said, "I'm only eight years old, and I need a dad! Would you *please* hurry up and get married again and get me one?"

Other children may pull away from the grieving child, just as adults pull away from one another. They may even treat the death lightly or ridicule the child for having only one parent. Although that is unfortunate, it is not as cruel as it sounds. Children do that because they are afraid that they, too, might lose a parent. I had the feeling of people treating me as though I had a contagious disease. In reality, that is just what it feels like. Children especially are afraid they'll "catch it." Explaining that to the hurt child may not take away the pain, but it will help to put the behavior into perspective.

Children feel grief too, but we must remember that they are not miniature adults. They have to work through their grief at their own level of understanding. One resource that really helped me recognize the unique aspects of children's grief was Eda LeShan's book *Learning to Say Good-Bye: When a Parent Dies* (New York: Avon, 1978). Older children may benefit by reading it themselves, and younger children can bring out a lot of pent-up feelings just by talking to a grown-up about what they see happening in the pictures. Pictures often help children get in touch with emotions they may have difficulty naming. We can help by being honest in our own feelings and by providing them a safe and nonthreatening atmosphere in which to grieve.

CHAPTER NINE

I'd Rather Have Him Dead

They say, if a man put away his wife, and she go from him, and become another man's, shall he return unto her again? shall not that land be greatly polluted? but thou hast played the harlot with many lovers; yet return again to me, saith the Lord.

And I said after she had done all these things, Turn thou unto me. But she returned not.

Jeremiah 3:1, 7

I think it is interesting how the Lord often draws analogies between his relationship with Israel and common human relationships with which people can identify. Though he speaks of Israel "as a wife [who] treacherously departeth from her husband" (Jeremiah 3:20), the analogy could exchange the pronouns *he* and *she* and be equally applicable.

In my dealings with divorced people, both professionally and personally, I have heard time and time again, "I would rather have him (or her) dead than with someone else."

Do the divorced grieve? Yes, they certainly do. In fact, because of the stigma of divorce that still exists in our culture, they often have a particularly difficult time dealing with grief because they lack the socially acceptable outlets of the widowed. In addition, the divorced often do not understand that grieving is, in fact, what they are experiencing. There is a certain amount of sympathy automatically built into the widowing process, but who holds a funeral service for a dead marriage?

Drs. Thomas H. Holmes and Monoru Masuda, writing in

Psychology Today (1972), tell us that life changes produce stress. On a scale of 1 to 100, the death of a spouse is rated 100. The only event even close to that is divorce at 73. To give you some idea of the effect of those numbers, compare them to the 63 rating of a jail term, the 47 of being fired, and the 30 of foreclosure of a mortgage. Being suddenly single after having once been married is a traumatic and overpowering event. Such losses trigger grief.

Let's look at the grieving process as it relates to divorced people. I've never experienced divorce, but I have come to know many who have. Listening to them share their divorce experiences, I have seen that the stages of grief in the handling of pain associated with divorce closely parallels the grieving of bereavement.

1. *Shock and denial.* There is an old saying that "the spouse is the last to know." Regardless of the reason for the divorce, that is often true. The spouse doesn't want to know. There is a false sense of security in denial. How many divorced people have expressed their total shock and

disbelief when confronted with a mate who wanted to terminate the marriage? How many have said, "I knew our marriage wasn't perfect, but I never thought things were that bad!" Later they, like the widowed, go over and over in their minds the circumstances. "Why was it that bad? What could I have done differently?"

2. *Guilt.* The guilt involved in a divorce is often monumental. Each party feels a certain sense of responsibility for the failure of the marriage. Even the ones who consider themselves the victims of the situation will feel guilty, wondering, "What did I do to drive him away?" or "What should I have done to make her happy?"

3. *Anger.* For the divorced person, anger is a very difficult part of the process because the objects of that anger are often close at hand. The divorced have to cope with a physically absent though emotionally ubiquitous ex-spouse, as well as children, former in-laws, friends, and family who may well have gotten involved in the whole situation.

4. *Depression.* You don't have to be single to feel

depressed. All of us feel that way at one time or another. But depression is a major aspect of healing from divorce for all of the same reasons it is a part of grieving the death of a loved one. When we lose a part of ourselves, by whatever circumstance, we will mourn our loss. It is normal, for a while at least, to feel very sorry for ourselves.

5. *Resolution.* Grief over a divorce can be resolved just as grief over a death can be. You've probably heard it said that time heals all wounds. Well, I'm here to tell you that it's not the time that does the healing; it's what we do with the time. We all know people many years into their singleness who are as raw in their grief as if it happened yesterday. When we talk to them, we can hear the pain and feel the tension. Like an overwound clock spring ready to explode, they infuse the air around them with their bitterness.

Hanging on to guilt and anger and even depression is self-defeating in the extreme. These emotions, nourished and embraced, will grow like a cancer until they consume

their host. The treatment for any cancer is painful and debil-
itating, but the alternative is worse.

To those who are going through this experience, I would
say: Let it go. Forgive those who have harmed you, and forgive yourself. Look carefully at the process through which
you are going. If you find yourself stuck in one of the stages,
then get yourself unstuck. Talk to others who have successfully gone through what you are experiencing. (The key word
here is *successfully*. Not every person who has known grief
has been successful in resolving it. The number of years a
person has been alone is irrelevant if he or she is still emotionally crippled by the loss.)

Take a class. Read a book. Participate in activities with
others who have a value system similar to your own; you can
help and support one another. Seek counsel through the
priesthood channels of the Church. The bishop, as a judge in
Israel, holds the keys to your healing spiritually and also
emotionally, should you need counseling through the
Church's social services agency. If you do seek professional

help on your own, choose your counselor wisely. Make sure he or she is a person who will understand and respect your values. You're already trying to cope with a life that is as unbalanced as a mobile with one component missing. You don't want someone to guide you down a path even more out of line with where you feel you should be going. Each of us must rebalance our own life in harmony with our own values. We should not attempt to homogeneously blend with someone else's ideal.

Seek outside help quickly if you feel suicidal, unable to cope, stuck and unable to move, or have physical symptoms, such as extreme weight loss, that do not abate with time.

I think Shakespeare said it nicely when, through the character of Polonius in *Hamlet,* he counseled, "This above all, to thine own self be true. And it must follow as the night the day, thou canst not then be false to any man." Be honest with yourself. Grief is hard work. Get at it. Do it. Move. Heal. Grow.

CHAPTER TEN

I Don't Know What to Say

Ye are desirous to come into the fold of God, and to be called his people, and are willing to bear one another's burdens, that they may be light; yea, and are willing to mourn with those that mourn; yea, and comfort those that stand in need of comfort.

Mosiah 18:8–9

OCTOBER 3, 1982

A really special thing happened the other day. I got a card in the mail from Joanne. It said, "I've been wanting to write or to call, but I just didn't know what to say. I guess I just want you to know that I'm thinking about you and I love you."

I wrote back to her that very day and said, "Joanne, you said exactly the right thing. Thank you."

*I*t's a helpless feeling. Someone you love is hurting. You want to help, you really do; but you don't know what to say or to do. Everything that comes to your mind somehow seems trite and inadequate. So you either stumble around and say all those trite, empty, worse-than-useless words, or you don't say anything at all.

I watched the helplessness of my friends in those early days. I think that a major part of the problem lies in a lack of understanding of the grief process. They didn't know what I was going through, so they couldn't relate to my pain. I didn't know what was happening either, except that it hurt worse than any physical or mental pain that I had ever experienced before. When I'd try to explain what I was feeling, it frightened people. They couldn't handle it emotionally and so they would back away from me, which left me feeling isolated, angry, and hurt.

If you know someone who is bereaved and you want to know what to say and do, here are some suggestions gleaned from many different sources, including personal experience.

The first, and hardest, step is to confront your own feelings about death. We truly are a death-denying society, and most of us have little direct experience with dying. We know it only in the abstract and at a distance. But if you want to help a grieving person, you cannot do it from an emotional distance or in the abstract. You have to get up close. That will be difficult if you are not in touch with your own feelings. Intense emotional pain is involved in grief, and if you do get close enough to help, you will be close enough to feel part of that pain. Allow yourself to be human and to feel.

It's not wrong to express your own grief while comforting

the bereaved. Some of the people who had been closest to me before the death avoided me after the death because they would not risk the pain. "If we come," they'd say, "we'll be no help to you. We'd just bawl right along with you." But that would have been just the help I needed! Some of the kindest expressions of condolence I received were from people who did nothing more than put their arms around me and cry with me. So let yourself feel, and don't be afraid of death's shadow.

Learn what you can about the grieving process. Do not learn about grieving so that you can be cold and clinical and have your head filled with a lot of facts and statistics; rather, do it so that when you see a bereaved person exhibiting anger or guilt or shock, you will understand that these things are a normal part of the grieving process.

For me, the hardest part of grieving was dealing with the anger. Many people shut me out because they overreacted to my feelings and emotions during this stage of grieving. They were expecting me to handle my anger from the same position of strength and self-control that I had been able to cultivate in other parts of my life. But I was not operating from a position of strength.

My whole world was rocking on its foundations, and I was angry about that. It would have been so helpful to have had friends, family, and church leaders who understood and gave me their permission to own my anger, as well as some realistic help on what to do with my anger. When I came to know myself, I did those things for myself. But even then, when I tried to explain that to others, they did not understand.

Just a few weeks ago, my ward Relief Society president attended a workshop on bereavement. She told me later how she sat, with tears in her eyes, thinking of all the things my ward had done that were well-intentioned but counterproductive because they had not understood what was happening to me and had not really listened when I tried to tell them.

Be physically present. A lot of support systems are in

operation for the bereaved prior to and immediately following the funeral, but they tend to drop off after a few weeks.
Just about the time the mourner's protective cocoon of shock
is fading and the real pain is beginning, the support evapo-
rates. Because we are in shock during those early days before
and after the funeral, we may appear to be a lot stronger
than we really are. Don't be deceived and walk away from the
bereaved too early. It got very lonely for me to receive, in lieu
of comfort, pats on the back and reminders of how strong I
was. One young widow with several small children became
very tired of hearing how well she was taking her husband's
death. She said she wanted to tell everybody to call her up at
midnight and listen to her scream.

*Don't worry that you don't have the answers when the
bereaved ask you, "Why?"* I think one reason people avoid
mourners is that they think they have to give some sort of
explanation: "It's God's will." "She's so much better off now."
"At least he's not suffering anymore." Believe it or not, these
things offer very little comfort to the grieving person. Be

honest. Admit that you don't know why, that you don't have the answers.

Elizabeth Kubler-Ross, in dealing with the terminally ill, used to tell her patients that she felt helpless or at a loss for words. Then she listened quietly and waited for a cue from the patient. That same process works with the mourner. Share and feel together.

Sometimes all you have to do is just be there and let people know that they are safe with you, that they can say anything they need to say, that they can cry in your presence, without fear of ridicule or judgment.

Learn the difference between sympathy and empathy and be empathic. Sympathy says, "You poor thing. Isn't life the pits? And there you are, so helpless and unable to get out of it." Nobody wants to be pitied. Empathy says, "I love you. I care. I'm with you." Empathy is encouraging. It is recognizing that grief is a natural process of confronting and adjusting to death and that each person holds the keys to his or her own healing. Empathy is walking a moon in someone else's moccasins. Sympathy wallows. Empathy lifts.

Listen empathically. Hear the unspoken as well as the spoken word. Observe the body language. Don't block the emotion being expressed by pulling away either verbally or with your own body language. Allow the person to own his or her sorrow, anger, despair, or guilt. If a person is raging at you with anger, don't take it personally. Make it clear that you've heard the message. You might say, "I can see that you're really angry. I'd probably be angry too." Don't say, "I know how you feel," unless you honestly do. Let the person know it's okay to feel angry or guilty or upset in your presence.

Don't be frightened by silences. A lot of processing goes on in the mind. Watch the eyes and the hands. You can see that something is happening. Just be there.

Don't be afraid to touch if it seems appropriate. Take your cue from the mourner. If you touch and the person pulls away from you, he or she doesn't want to be touched. If the person responds, then continue. Many times I felt so starved for physical contact that a warm hug was exactly what I needed. But don't force yourself to touch if you don't feel a desire to. It will come across as stiff and artificial, worse than no contact at all.

Don't be afraid of questions and doubts. Sometimes we feel that if a person has enough faith or a strong enough testimony, he or she won't feel doubts. Nonsense! Someone's whole world has been torn apart: that's a faith-shaking experience. Now, the person usually puts his or her world (and testimony) back together much stronger than it was before, but the process is not without its moments of doubt and fear. Don't be deceived by the public face of the bereaved. Accept the questioning and don't expect the person to be coming from the stance of assurance from which you are operating. Have a little faith in yourself. The outpourings of the Spirit are tremendously strong during bereavement. The moments of doubt are countered by dramatic flashes of pure knowledge.

Keep the Spirit with you and follow its counsel; the mourner will feel it too.

Don't try to force the person to talk or to cry. Some people have trouble getting in touch with their emotions. Letting them know that they can do so in your presence is more a condition of who you are to them rather than what you say to them. Such things should never, never be forced.

Don't avoid the subject of the deceased. The mourner may get a little misty, but he or she will know you care. You don't have to dredge up the memory whenever you're with the person but don't walk around on eggs to avoid it, either. Bring up pleasant, good memories of the deceased.

Don't avoid the mourning person. Bereavement is a lonely and painful time. The living one has lost his or her intimate other half and needs human contact. Some people think that love and hate are opposites. I guess that from a strictly semantic point of view, they are. But from an emotional point of view, people would rather be loved or hated than ignored. That's the true dichotomy. To avoid the mourner just because you might share some pain together is a gross injustice.

Remember that the grieving process is a lengthy one. There are no pills for instant adjustment. The funeral is the beginning of grief, not the ending. The worst anger, guilt, and depression may come months after the death. Take time for a personal visit. Make a quick phone call. Send a little note. You don't have to say anything profound. Just say, "I'm thinking about you. I care. I love you." My Relief Society visiting teacher did not miss a single week in many months following my husband's death. She called at least once a week just to say, "Hi, how are you?" Be particularly sensitive to the special days: holidays, birthdays, wedding anniversaries, and the anniversary of death. Be there and follow the lead of the bereaved person.

My parents drove all the way from Nevada to be with me on the first anniversary of Carmon's death. On several occasions, while I was talking with friends on the phone, those friends could sense that I was upset and would say, "Do you need me? I'll be right there!"

Be aware that grieving consumes immense emotional energy. Psychologists tell us that one hour of emotional stress is as draining as three hours of hard physical labor. The mourner's only reality is that world of pain inside. He or she will live only for and through that pain for a long while. Anything you can do to help ease the load will be helpful. Recognize that people in mourning are preoccupied with their grief and won't be up to their usual level of performance professionally, personally, or spiritually. Sometimes we tend to want to get them out or "keep them busy so they won't think so much." But they need to think, and all of the emotional energy going into the introspection will lead to the eventual resolution of grief. It is counterproductive to load someone up with dozens of projects at a time when just washing the face seems a monumental achievement.

Help with the practical things. A recent issue of *Reader's Digest* featured an article about a neighbor who appeared on the doorstep of a bereaved family prepared to shine their shoes. I remember a friend showing up with her apron on. "I'm not much on words," she explained, "but I can clean."

Another example of help with practical needs occurred on the anniversary of my husband's death, which coincided with the first week of school. When the teacher in the next room looked in and found me at my desk staring into space, she came over with cutouts for my bulletin boards and some first-of-the-year activities that had been photocopied and were ready for me to use. Practical help doesn't have to be enormously time-consuming, monumental, or accompanied by fanfare. The little things will be most appreciated and remembered.

Don't take it upon yourself to "get rid of the memories." The mourner will know when he or she can put away clothing or pictures. It took me more than a year before I had the strength to sort through my husband's clothing, but I would have resented someone else's doing it for me.

Do not judge in the case of a death by suicide. I admit that suicide is an area of which I have little knowledge or experience. The only practical suggestion I offer is to refrain from judging. Only the Lord can judge what is in a person's heart. The surviving family of a suicide victim need, if anything, even more comfort and support. They experience the shock, anger, guilt, and depression in monumental proportions. All of the other suggestions made thus far also apply: be present, be real, care, listen, and don't judge.

Be cognizant that outside help may be needed. If, after learning about the grieving process, you sense that the bereaved person is stuck in the grief; if a lot of time has passed without resolution; if there are some serious physical symptoms, such as an extreme weight loss or talk of suicide, consider recommending outside help. In addition to one-on-one professional counseling, classes in bereavement are taught at many universities and colleges; support groups are another valuable resource available in many cities. If you cannot locate one in your area, write for information about starting one. For the widowed, write to THEOS Foundation,

1301 Clark Building, 717 Liberty Avenue, Penn Hills Mall, Pittsburgh, PA 15222, phone (412) 471-7779. For bereaved parents, write to The Compassionate Friends, Inc., P.O. Box 3696, Oak Brook, IL 60522-3696, phone (708) 990-0010, and fax (708) 990-0246.

If you are in a position that puts you in frequent contact with bereaved persons, whether in a professional or a spiritual capacity, consider taking a course or workshop on death and dying. It may be the beginning of the greatest journey you'll ever make, a journey of understanding and peace within yourself.

Epilogue

Therefore being justified by faith, we have peace with God through our Lord Jesus Christ: by whom also we have access by faith into this grace wherein we stand, and rejoice in hope of the glory of God. And not only so, but we glory in tribulations also: knowing that tribulation worketh patience; and patience, experience; and experience, hope.

Romans 5:1–4

DECEMBER 1, 1983

I can't believe I've been keeping this journal for over a year!

Today is my thirty-ninth birthday. I'm finally Jack Benny's age!

I spent the day in Tucson with our fifth-graders from school. I wasn't looking forward to it, but it was much nicer than last year's trip. I remember being an emotional wreck by the time I got home last year. In fact, I cried all the way home on the bus, feigning sleep so as not to upset the children. You see, I bore the weight of knowing that Carm had planned to go on that trip, and his not being there reinforced for me that he was dead. I hadn't realized how much it had weighed on me until today, when I took the same trip without that burden. I feel so alive and whole and healed. What a joy to my spirit!

Mom came down a few weeks ago and helped me to clean house. It took a full year to get there, but I finally went through all of Carmon's clothes and personal belongings. I selected carefully the memories I wanted to keep for myself, and the children chose theirs. Then Carm's brother came and took what clothing, tools, and such that he wanted. The rest went to Deseret Industries or the dump. These past months I've felt impressed to strip down to traveling weight. I don't know why; I just know that I need to obey that impression. It may be that the only traveling I'll be doing is to go forward within myself.

I think I am going forward too. The past is a nice place to visit; but after all this time, I no longer want to live there. I don't know what is in the future for me, and I'm a little bit frightened of it. But I do know I'm going toward it, whatever it is. Opening my heart to new experiences means risking further pain; but without risk, there is no growth, and without growth, there is no faith nor hope nor love nor joy.

It was funny the other night; I was driving to the singles conference and talking to the Lord as I sometimes do. Suddenly I found myself thanking Him for the pain and for His "tough love" that shook me from my complacency and made me grow. I thanked Him for the tough laws, too, the ones that are so hard to live sometimes—tithing, which allows me to earn such blessings from heaven that my children, though fatherless, have never had to want; chastity, which has schooled me in a power and strength I cannot even describe, and which secures for me relationships with close friends that are uplifting because they don't mistake thrills for joy or tinsel for treasure; prayer, which can be a thirty-second spot-check or an intense two-way dialogue, depending on my effort; fasting, through which come answers beyond my mortal ken; scriptures, which quiet my troubled heart; journal writing, which clarifies my confused soul.

Yes, I do feel whole again. I have learned that in resolution of grief the goal is to be whole again, to look forward and not backward, to reinvest emotional energy in growth and not in memories. But it never means to forget, and it never means no longer to love, for the love and the memory are always there to keep and to ponder in my heart. To take grief out of death is to take love out of life.